Cats

Cats

Edited by
Lynn Hughes

CONGDON & LATTÈS
New York

A cat came dancing out of a barn
With a pair of bag-pipes under her arm;
She could sing nothing but, Fiddle cum fee,
The mouse has married the bumble-bee.
Pipe, cat; dance, mouse;
We'll have a wedding at our good house.

NURSERY RHYME

5

When the tea is brought at five o'clock,
And all the neat curtains are drawn with care,
The little black cat with bright green eyes
Is suddenly purring there.
At first she pretends, having nothing to do,
She has come in merely to blink by the grate,
But though tea may be late
Or the milk may be sour,
She is never late.
The white saucer like some full moon descends
At last from the cloud of the table above;
She sighs and dreams and thrills and glows,
Transfigured with love.
She nestles over the shining rim,
Buries her chin in the creamy sea;
Her tail hangs loose; each drowsy paw
Is doubled under each bending knee.
A long dim ecstasy holds her life;
Her world is an infinite shapeless white,
Till her tongue has curled the last holy drop
Then she sinks back into the night,
Draws and dips her body to heap
Her sleepy nerves in the great arm-chair,
Lies defeated and buried deep
Three or four hours unconscious there.

HAROLD MONRO
MILK FOR THE CAT

In October not even a cat is to be found in London.

ANON

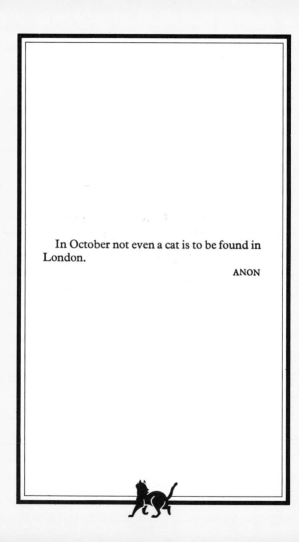

Half loving-kindness and half disdain
    Thou comest to my call serenely suave,
With humming speech and gracious gestures
    grave,
    In salutation courtly and urbane:

Yet must I humble me thy grace to gain –
    For wiles may win thee, but no arts enslave,
    And nowhere gladly thou abidest save
Where naught disturbs the concord of thy
    reign.

Sphinx of my quiet hearth! who deignst to
    dwell
    Friend of my toil, companion of mine ease
    Thine is the love of Ra and Rameses;
That men forget dost thou remember well,
Beholden still in blinking reveries,
With sombre sea-green gaze inscrutable.

GRAHAM R. TOMSON
LE CHAT NOIR

When rats infest the Palace a lame cat is better than the swiftest horse.

CHINESE PROVERB

C c

For I will consider my Cat Jeoffrey.

For he is the servant of the Living God, duly and daily serving him.

For having consider'd God and himself he will consider his neighbour.

For if he meets another cat he will kiss her in kindness.

For when he takes his prey he plays with it to give it a chance.

For when his day's work is done his business more properly begins.

For he keeps the Lord's watch in the night against the adversary.

For he counteracts the powers of darkness by his electrical skin & glaring eyes.

For in his morning orisons he loves the sun and the sun loves him.

For he is of the tribe of Tiger.

For he will not do destruction, if he is well fed, neither will he spit without provocation.

For he purrs in thankfulness, when God tells him he's a good Cat.

For he is an instrument for the children to learn benevolence upon.

For every house is incomplete without him.

CHRISTOPHER SMART
JUBILATE AGNO

I love little pussy, her coat is so warm;
And if I don't hurt her, she'll do me no harm.
So I'll not pull her tail, nor drive her away,
But pussy and I very gently will play.
She shall sit by my side, and I'll give her
   some food;
And she'll love me because I am gentle and
   good.

I'll pat pretty pussy, and then she will purr;
And thus show her thanks for my kindness to
   her.
But I'll not pinch her ears, nor tread on her
   paw,
Lest I should provoke her to use her sharp
   claw.
I never will vex her, nor make her displeased –
For pussy don't like to be worried and teased.

ANON

On the sheep-cropped summit, under hot sun,
The mouse crouched, staring out the chance
It dared not take.

                Time and a world
Too old to alter, the five mile prospect —
Woods, villages, farms — hummed its heat-
   heavy
Stupor of life.

                Whether to two
Feet or four, how are prayers contracted!
Whether in God's eye or the eye of a cat.

TED HUGHES
CAT AND MOUSE

Alice was a little startled by seeing the Cheshire Cat sitting on a bough of a tree a few yards off. The Cat only grinned when it saw Alice. It looked good-natured, she thought: still it had *very* long claws and a great many teeth, so she felt that it ought to be treated with respect. 'Cheshire Puss,' she began, rather timidly, as she did not at all know whether it would like the name: however, it only grinned a little wider. *Then it faded and disappeared.* Alice waited a little, half expecting to see it again, but it did not appear, and after a minute or two she walked on in the direction in which the March Hare was said to live. She paused, she looked up, and there was the Cat again, sitting on a branch of a tree. 'Did you say pig, or fig?' said the Cat. 'I said pig,' replied Alice; 'and I wish you wouldn't keep appearing and vanishing so suddenly: you make one quite giddy.' 'All right,' said the Cat; and this time it vanished quite slowly, beginning with the end of the tail, and ending with the grin, which remained some time after the rest of it had gone. 'Well! I've often seen a cat without a grin,' thought Alice; 'but a grin without a cat! It's the most curious thing I ever saw in all my life!'

LEWIS CARROLL
ALICE IN WONDERLAND

She had a name among the children;
But no one loved though someone owned
Her, locked her out of doors at bedtime
And had her kittens duly drowned.

In Spring, nevertheless, this cat
Ate blackbirds, thrushes, nightingales,
And birds of bright voice and plume and flight,
As well as scraps from neighbours' pails.

I loathed and hated her for this;
One speckle on a thrush's breast
Was worth a million such; and yet
She lived long, till God gave her rest.

EDWARD THOMAS
A CAT

And all the sailors and the Admirals cried,
When they saw him nearing the further side, –
'He has gone to fish, for his Aunt Jobiska's
'Runcible Cat with crimson whiskers'.

EDWARD LEAR
THE POBBLE WHO HAD NO TOES

It is reported that the flesh of Cats salted and sweetened hath power in it to draw wens from the body, and being warmed to cure the Hemmorhoids and pains in the veins and back, according to the Verse of Ursinus. In Spain and Gallia Norbon, they eat Cats, but first of all take away their head and tail, and hang the prepared flesh a night or two in the open cold air, to exhale the savour of it, finding the flesh thereof almost as sweet as a cony. The flesh of Cats can seldom be free from poison, by reason of their daily food, eating Rats and Mice, Wrens and other birds which feed on poison, and above all the brain of the Cat is most venomous, for it being above all measure dry, stoppeth the animal spirits, that they cannot pass into the venticle, by reason thereof memory faileth, and the infected person falleth into a Phrenzie. The hair also of a Cat being eaten unawares, stoppeth the artery and causeth suffocation. To conclude this point it appeareth that this is a dangerous beast, and that therefore as for necessity we are constrained to nourish them for the suppressing of small vermin: so with a wary eye we must avoid their harms, making more account of their use than of their persons.

EDWARD TOPSELL
THE HISTORY OF FOUR-FOOTED BEASTS

The value of a cat which guards a king's barn, if it is killed or stolen: its head is to be put downwards on an even clean floor, and its tail is held up, and wheat is poured about it until the tip of its tail be covered. Unless the grains can be obtained, its value is a milch sheep with her lamb and her wool. The worth of another cat is four legal pence.

The attributes of a cat and of every animal the milk of which people do not drink, are valued at a third of its worth, or the worth of its litter.

Whoever shall sell a cat, let him guarantee it free from caterwauling every moon, and that it do not devour its kittens, and that it have ears, eyes, teeth and claws, and that it be a good mouser.

HYWEL DDA
THE LAW (10th CENTURY)

Within that porch, across the way,
  I see two naked eyes this night;
Two eyes that neither shut nor blink,
  Searching my face with a green light.

But cats to me are strange, so strange —
  I cannot sleep if one is near;
And though I'm sure I see those eyes,
  I'm not so sure a body's there!

W. H. DAVIES
THE CAT

Cat! who hast pass'd thy grand climacteric,
  How many mice and rats hast in thy days
  Destroy'd? How many tit bits stolen? Gaze
With those bright languid segments green, and
  prick
Those velvet ears – but pr'ythee do not stick
  Thy latent talons in me – and upraise
  Thy gentle mew – and tell me all thy frays,
Of fish and mice, and rats and tender chick.
Nay, look not down, nor lick thy dainty
  wrists –
  For all thy wheezy asthma – and for all
Thy tail's tip is nick'd off – and though the fists
  Of many a maid have given thee many a
  maul,
Still is that fur as soft, as when the lists
  In youth thou enter'dest on glass bottled
  wall.

JOHN KEATS
TO MRS REYNOLDS' CAT

I am sorry, my little cat, I am sorry –
if I had it, you should have it;
but there is a war on.

No, there are no table-scraps;
there was only an omelette
made from dehydrated eggs,
and baked apples to follow, and we finished it
    all.
The butcher has no lights,
the fishmonger has no cod's heads –
there is nothing for you
but cat-biscuit
and those remnants of yesterday's ham;
you must do your best with it.

Round and pathetic eyes,
baby mouth opened in a reproachful cry,
how can I explain to you?
I know, I know:
'Mistress, it is not nice;
the ham is very salt
and the cat-biscuit very dull,
I sniffed at it, and the smell was not enticing.
Do you not love me any more?'

DOROTHY L. SAYERS
WAR CAT

There was a crooked man, and he went a
    crooked mile
He found a crooked sixpence against a crooked
    stile
He bought a crooked cat, which caught a
    crooked mouse
And they all lived together in a little crooked
    house.

NURSERY RHYME

There is a propensity belonging to common house-cats that is very remarkable; I mean their violent fondness for fish, which appears to be their most favourite food: and yet nature in this instance seems to have planted in them an appetite that, unassisted, they know not how to gratify: for of all quadrupeds cats are the least disposed towards water; and will not, when they can avoid it, deign to wet a foot, much less to plunge into that element.

Quadrupeds that prey on fish are amphibious: such is the otter, which by nature is so well formed for diving, that it makes great havoc among the inhabitants of the waters. Not supposing that we had any of those beasts in our shallow brooks, I was much pleased to see a male otter, brought to me, weighing twenty-one pounds, that had been shot on the bank of our stream below the Priory, where the rivulet divides the parish of Selborne from Harteley Wood.

GILBERT WHITE
NATURAL HISTORY OF SELBORNE

Diddlety, diddlety, dumpty
The cat ran up the plum tree;
Half a crown
To fetch her down
Diddlety, diddlety, dumpty.

NURSERY RHYME

Wildcats grow to an enormous size, at least double that of the very largest domestic cat. It is comparatively rarely that one sees the animals themselves in the daytime, for they are creatures of the dark and the starlight. Once I caught one accidentally in a rabbit snare, a vast tom with ten rings to his tail, and that first year at Camusfearna I twice saw the kittens at play in the dawn, frolicking among the primroses and budding birch on the bank beyond the croft wall. They looked beautiful, very soft and fluffy, and almost gentle; there was no hint of the ferocity that takes a heavy toll of lambs and red-deer calves. Before man exterminated the rabbits they were the staple food both of the big leggy hill foxes and of these low-ground wildcats, and every morning I would see the heavily indented pad-marks in the sand at the burrow mouths. But now the rabbits have gone and the lambs are still here in their season, and where there has been a strong lamb at dusk, at dawn there are raw bones and a fleece like a bloodstained swab in a surgery.

GAVIN MAXWELL
RING OF BRIGHT WATER

We are all in the dumps,
For diamonds are trumps;
The kittens are gone to St Paul's.
The babies are bit,
The Moon's in a fit,
And the houses are built without walls.

ANON

She moved through the garden in glory,
    because
She had very long claws at the end of her paws.
Her back was arched, her tail was high,
A green fire glared in her vivid eye;
And all the Toms, though never so bold,
Quailed at the martial Marigold.

RICHARD GARNETT
MARIGOLD

Of all God's creatures there is only one that cannot be made the slave of the lash. That one is the cat. If man could be crossed with the cat it would improve man, but it would deteriorate the cat.

MARK TWAIN
NOTEBOOK

The Cat keeps his side of the bargain . . . He will kill mice, and he will be kind to Babies when he is in the house, just so long as they do not pull his tail too hard. But when he has done that, and between times, and when the moon gets up and night comes, he is the Cat that walks by himself, and all places are alike to him. Then he goes out to the Wet Wild Woods or up on the Wet Wild Trees or on the Wet Wild Roofs, waving his wild tail and walking by his wild lone.

RUDYARD KIPLING
THE CAT THAT WALKED BY HIMSELF

Picture acknowledgements

5 Sara Midda. A Cat Came Dancing Out of a Barn.

7 Lucy Su. Tabby Ambush. *Michael Parkin Fine Art*.

9 Cats Dressed Up. *Mary Evans Picture Library*.

11 John Bold. Portrait of a Cat. *Manchester City Art Gallery*.

13 Edward Lear. Cat.

15 Henri Rousseau. Portrait of Pierre Loti (detail). *Kunsthaus Zurich*.

17 The Flirt. *Mary Evans Picture Library*.

19 Toko. Cat. *The Metropolitan Museum of Art. Gift in memory of Charles Stewart Smith*, 1914.

21 Tenniel. The Cheshire Cat. *Mary Evans Picture Library*.

23 Egyptian wall painting (detail). *Michael Holford Library*.

25 Martin Leman. Camilla.

27 Edward Topsell. Cat. *The History of Four-Footed Beasts*.

29 Randolph Caldecott. The House that Jack Built (detail).

31 Justin Todd. Macavity.

For permission to use copyright material we are indebted to the following:

Jonathan Cape Ltd for 'The Cat' by W. H. Davies taken from *The Complete Poems of W. H. Davies*; Gerald Duckworth & Co Ltd for 'Milk for the Cat' by Harold Monro from *The Collected Poems of Harold Monro*; Faber & Faber Ltd for 'Cat and Mouse' by Ted Hughes from *Lupercal*; G. G. Harrap & Co Ltd for 'The War Cat' by Dorothy Sayers from *The Poet's Cat – An Anthology by Mona Gooden*; Littlebrown & Co for 'Marigold' by Richard Garnett from *The Cat in Verse*; Liverpool University Press for an extract from *The Law of Hywel Dda*; Macmillan & Co, London for an extract from *Alice in Wonderland* by Lewis Carroll; The National Trust of Great Britain for an extract from *The Cat that Walked by Himself* by Rudyard Kipling, published by Macmillan & Co, London; Penguin Books Ltd for an extract from *Ring of Bright Water* by Gavin Maxwell; Myfanwy Thomas for 'A Cat' by Edward Thomas from *Collected Poems* published by Faber & Faber Ltd.